HIP-HOP HEADLINERS

D0864783

MARY J. BLIGE

Gareth Stevens
Publishing

By Sofia Z. Maimone

Please visit our Web site, www.garethstevens.com. For a free color catalog of all our high-quality books, call toll free 1-800-542-2595 or fax 1-877-542-2596.

Library of Congress Cataloging-in-Publication Data

Maimone, Sofia Z.
  Mary J. Blige / Sofia Z. Maimone.
     p. cm. — (Hip-hop headliners)
  Includes bibliographical references and index.
  ISBN 978-1-4339-4804-6 (library binding)
  ISBN 978-1-4339-4805-3 (pbk.)
  ISBN 978-1-4339-4806-0 (6-pack)
  1. Blige, Mary J.—Juvenile literature. 2. Rap musicians—United States—Biography—
Juvenile literature. I. Title.
  ML3930.B585M35 2011
  782.421643092—dc22
  [B]
                                        2010027405

First Edition

Published in 2011 by
Gareth Stevens Publishing
111 East 14th Street, Suite 349
New York, NY 10003

Copyright © 2011 Gareth Stevens Publishing

Designer: Haley W. Harasymiw
Editor: Therese Shea

Photo credits: Cover, pp. 2–32 (background) Shutterstock.com; cover (Mary J. Blige), p. 1 Stephen Lovekin/Getty Images; p. 5 Larry Busacca/Getty Images; pp. 7, 17 Frank Micelotta/ Image Direct; pp. 9, 25 Vince Bucci/Getty Images; p. 11 Theo Wargo/Getty Images; p. 13 Kevin Winter/Getty Images; p. 15 Arnold Turner/WireImage; pp. 19, 21 Scott Gries/Getty Images; p. 23 Brad Barket/Getty Images; p. 27 Michael Loccisano/Getty Images; p. 29 Astrid Stawiarz/Getty Images.

Printed in the United States of America

CPSIA compliance information: Batch #CW11GS: For further information contact Gareth Stevens, New York, New York at 1-800-542-2595.

Contents

Powerful Hip-Hop

Mary J. Blige is one of the most powerful hip-hop singers today.

Young Voice

Mary J. Blige was born in New York City on January 11, 1971. She lived in Savannah, Georgia, for a few years.

Mary, her mother, and her sister moved north again. They lived in Yonkers, New York. Mary had a sad childhood.

Mary was unhappy and angry.

She dropped out of high school.

One day, she made a recording of

herself singing.

Mary's stepfather gave the recording to a music business. They liked Mary's singing. Soon, she sang backup for other singers.

The Albums

In 1991, Mary began to work with Sean "Puffy" Combs. He helped Mary make her first album.

Sean Combs

Mary's first album was called *What's the 411?* Her songs were a mix of R&B and rap. No other singer was making songs like this.

In 1994, Mary's album *My Life* told of her hard life as a singer. With each album, Mary grew up a little more.

The 2001 album *No More Drama* showed a new side of Mary. She was ready to leave the past behind.

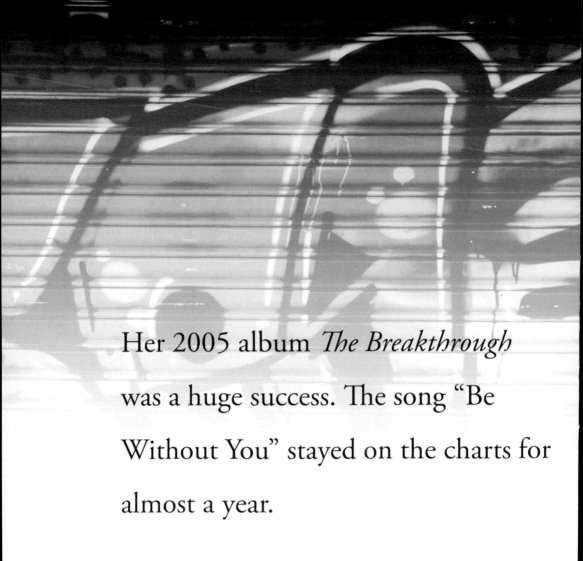

Her 2005 album *The Breakthrough* was a huge success. The song "Be Without You" stayed on the charts for almost a year.

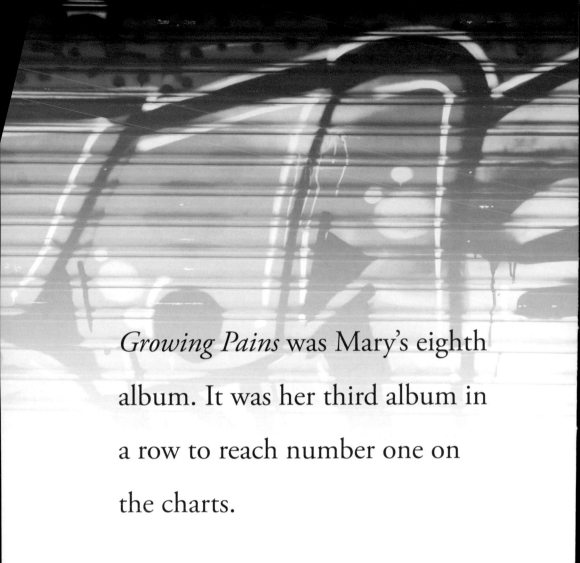

Growing Pains was Mary's eighth album. It was her third album in a row to reach number one on the charts.

25

A Stronger, Better Life

In 2007, Mary started a women's center in Yonkers, New York. She wants to help women become stronger. Mary helps them make their lives better.

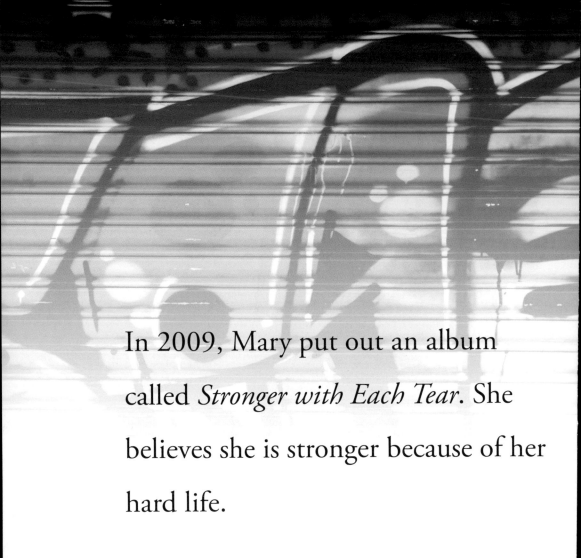

In 2009, Mary put out an album called *Stronger with Each Tear*. She believes she is stronger because of her hard life.

Timeline

1971   Mary is born on January 11 in New York City.

1991   Mary works with Sean Combs for the first time.

1992   Mary's album *What's the 411?* becomes a hit.

2001   *No More Drama* comes out.

2005   "Be Without You" hits the charts.

2007   Mary opens the Mary J. Blige Center for Women.

2009   *Stronger with Each Tear* comes out.

For More Information

Books:

Bailey, Diane. *Mary J. Blige*. New York, NY: Rosen Publishing Group, 2009.

Torres, Jennifer. *Mary J. Blige*. Hockessin, DE: Mitchell Lane Publishers, 2008.

Web Sites:

Mary J. Blige Biography
www.billboard.com/#/artist/mary-j-blige/bio/43746

The Mary J. Blige Center for Women
www.ffawn.org/?p=57

Glossary

backup: music or singing that goes along with the main music or singing

charts: lists of songs or albums that have sold well

childhood: the time of being a child

drama: happenings that have strong feelings and actions

R&B: a short way to say rhythm and blues. This kind of music has a strong beat and is sometimes sad.

recording: a copy of sounds

Index